MAKE YOUR OWN WORKING PA

STEAM ENGINE

MAKE YOUR OWN PAPER MACHINE SERIES

MAKE YOUR OWN WORKING PAPER STEAM ENGINE

KYLE WICKWARE

INSTRUCTIONS BY

JIM CALHOUN

HARPER & ROW, PUBLISHERS, New York
Cambridge, Philadelphia, San Francisco, London
Mexico City, São Paulo, Singapore, Sydney

 For information address Harper & Row, Publishers, Inc., 10 East 53rd Street, New York, N.Y. 10022. Published simultaneously in Canada by Fitzhenry & Whiteside Limited, Toronto.

FIRST EDITION

Design by Jennie Nichols/Function thru Form

Illustrations by Guilbert Gates/Function thru Form

ISBN: 0-06-096034-5

86 87 88 89 90 10 9 8 7 6 5 4 3 2 1

INTRODUCTION

The invention of a practical steam engine is considered by many to mark the beginning of the Industrial Revolution. The steam engine is a simple idea that changed the history of the world.

The steam engine uses the tremendous pressure of steam created when water is boiled to move a piston inside a cylinder. The piston is attached by a rod to a crankshaft which changes the back and forth motion of the piston into rotary motion. The use of this rotary motion as a power source enabled the steam engine to usher in the modern age.

As early as 1712, Thomas Newcomen, an English blacksmith, developed a steam engine that could be used to pump water. But, the first steam engine to be considered practical was developed in 1765 by Scotsman James Watt. Mr. Watt's engine was economical to operate and therefore the uses of the steam engine began to expand.

Since the 1800s and throughout this century, the basic steam engine has been continually improved. Higher pressures from hotter steam and such innovations as the compound cylinder, the pre-heater, and the re-heater, which allow the same steam to be used more than once, have kept the steam engine a useful and practical energy source to the present day.

The steam engine is in wide use today all over the world. It is best known in the form of the steam locomotive but it takes more modern forms as well. Its most modern form can be traced to the steam turbine invented in 1884 by Charles Parsons. The steam turbine in its simplest form is little more than a windmill which is turned not by the wind but by a breeze of high-pressure steam flowing through its blades.

The steam turbine, driven with steam generated by burning coal, is considered by many to be the most efficient method of generating electricity in use today. The nuclear submarine, which uses the heat of a nuclear reactor to produce steam to drive a turbine, is undoubtedly one of the greatest achievements of modern technology.

In this book you are invited to recreate, with your own hands, a very important element of history.

ABOUT THE STEAMLESS STEAMER

The model you are about to create is called a "steamless" steamer. It uses air pressure stored in a ballon in place of steam, but is in all other regards a real steam engine.

Air pressure is allowed into the cylinder of your engine by a valve. This pressure forces the piston inside the cylinder to move. The piston is connected by a piston rod to the crankshaft, which is forced by the movement of the piston and rod to rotate. When the piston has traveled the length of the cylinder and can be pushed no further by the air pressure, the momentum of the flywheel attached to the crankshaft causes the crankshaft to continue to rotate. The piston is forced to travel back to the beginning point and the air trapped in the cylinder is allowed to escape. This completes the cycle. At this point, the intake valve opens again and thus another cycle begins.

The design of the cylinder and valve of your engine is one of the oldest types. It is called a "wobble cylinder" because the cylinder wobbles, or moves, when the engine runs. The motion of the cylinder is used to operate the valve which allows air pressure to enter the cylinder and trapped air to escape. It is a simple idea that works well.

Your model is not a simulation but a real working engine that you should find both educational and entertaining.

CONSTRUCTION OF THE STEAMLESS STEAMER

CAUTION: THE CONSTRUCTION OF THIS KIT REQUIRES THE USE OF SHARP CUTTING TOOLS AND "SUPER GLUE." THESE TOOLS AND THIS TYPE OF GLUE CAN BE DANGEROUS IF NOT HANDLED CAREFULLY. ADULT SUPERVISION IS SUGGESTED.

MATERIALS AND TOOLS

Before starting construction, assemble the following items:

Rubber band: the type that comes on the newspaper. It should be thin and small, not the large flat type.

Paper clips (2): Just about any type will work well. You may also use piano wire of the same size; about six inches is needed.

Toothpick: a round wood type. Don't use a flat one. You may substitute the stem of a "Q-TIP" if it is made of wood.

Ballpoint pen: Choose one that has a standard straight refill, not a tapered one. This refill serves as a form for the valve holes and for making air tubes.

Needle: a large sewing type. This is used for transferring marks to the reverse side of the parts. You may also use the metal point of a drawing compass.

Hobby knife: The X-ACTO with a one-quarter-inch shaft is the proper size. A number-eleven blade is handy for cutting and scoring. You will use the handle for forming the cylinder. You may substitute a section of one-quarter-inch dowel that is smooth and straight.

Metal-edge ruler: This item is optional but is very handy because it can serve to guide your knife when cutting out or scoring parts. The metal edge prevents the hobby knife from cutting into the ruler. A cork-backed ruler is ideal to prevent knife from slipping.

Sandpaper: 150 grit; don't use a coarser grit as it won't leave a smooth surface.

Graphite: Powdered or flaked graphite is used for lubrication.

Balloons: nine-inch size. Better quality (heavier) balloons work much better. Try different brands to find which give the best results.

Paper glue: Almost any white paper glue will work well. Do not use clear fast-drying plastic model cement.

"Super glue": Most "super glues" will give good results.

Scissors: You need a good sharp pair. Cheap ones tend to tear rather than cut.

Pliers: Needle-nose are best. You will use them to cut and bend the paper clip. The type that incorporate "side cutters" are what you need.

Cutting board: A thick section of cardboard is ideal. It needs to be hard and flat to provide a good working surface for cutting and scoring and to protect your table top.

Waxed paper: for protection when using super glue.

IMPORTANT CONSTRUCTION TIPS

Rome wasn't built in a day and neither should your model be. Take your time and work carefully. After all, you are building your model for learning and enjoyment. Although your model kit has built into it an allowance for error, the construction tips that follow can make the difference between a model you will demonstrate proudly and one that functions and shows less than perfectly.

CUTTING

Most of your cutting is best done with scissors. But when narrow slots must be cut, the hobby knife works best.

When cutting out parts, cut in the center of the solid line.

Cut only solid lines. Do not cut dotted or dashed lines.

Before cutting out each part, it is helpful to use a pencil to transfer part numbers from the page to the back of the individual part. **This will allow you to identify the parts once you cut them out.**

Work in numerical order, cutting out only the parts needed for each step before beginning the next step.

SCORING AND BENDING

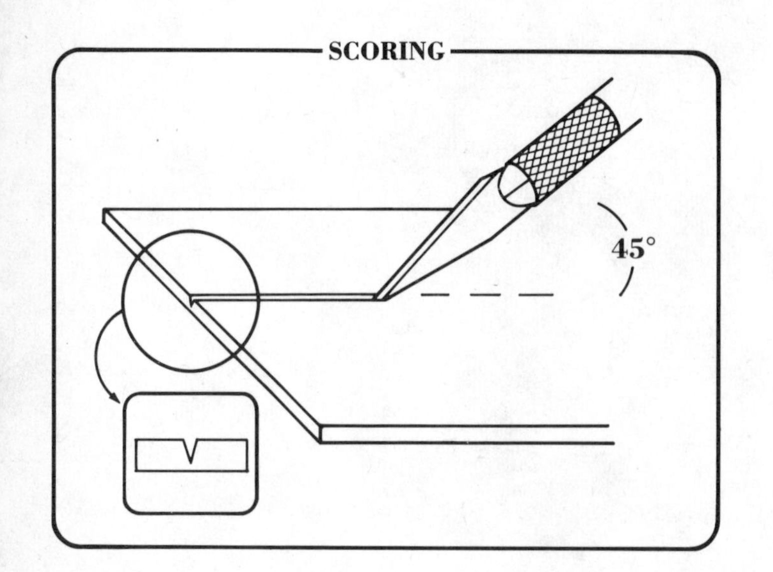

To make bending along dotted lines easier, first score lightly along the dotted line with your hobby knife. The easiest way to score is to use the back edge of the cutting blade of the hobby knife. This will prevent the possibility of cutting all the way through the paper. If you prefer, you may use the cutting edge of the knife to score. The idea is to cut halfway through the paper. Practice on some scrap paper before working on your model. Too much pressure on your knife will cut through the paper. When the paper bends with a clean open line, you have done the scoring right.

Once scoring of the part is complete, lay the part over the edge of a table top to make the initial bend. Next lift the part and continue bending past the 90-degree point. **You need to "overbend" the part so that when released it will have a natural tendency to stay at a 90-degree angle.**

USING PAPER GLUE

Always test for fit before gluing together the parts you have cut out. This gives you a chance to trim if needed.

Here is the best way to glue with white paper glue: First apply a few drops of glue to one of the two parts to be glued. Next spread the glue with a scrap piece of cardboard or paper. Leave only a thin film of glue. Paper absorbs the water in glue causing it to dry rather quickly. You may be surprised at just how quickly it dries. Hold the parts being glued together with your hands. (You are the clamp.) After about one minute, release the parts and check to see if the glue is holding. Apply pressure again if the glue is not yet dry. If the glue doesn't set in one minute, you are probably using too much glue.

USING "SUPER GLUE"

CAUTION: "SUPER GLUES" SHOULD BE HANDLED WITH EXTREME CARE. THEY ARE EXTREMELY DIFFICULT TO REMOVE FROM THE SKIN AND MAY IN FACT BOND SKIN TO SKIN. WHEN APPLYING SUPER GLUE TO A PART, ALWAYS HOLD THE PART BY WRAPPING A PIECE OF WAXED PAPER LOOSELY AROUND IT. THIS WILL HELP KEEP THE SUPER GLUE AWAY FROM YOUR SKIN. APPLY THIS GLUE IN VERY SMALL QUANTITIES TO AVOID SPILLING.

This glue helps make your model functional and long lasting. It also allows you to sand the paper where instructed without leaving a fuzzy surface. It is used on some holes to form a bearing surface where a metal shaft passes through paper.

Be sure to apply it where instructed; on bearing holes, rub areas on the cylinder to stiffen it.

You will use this glue to bond metal parts to paper as well. IT IS IMPORTANT TO ROUGH UP THE METAL SOMEWHAT WITH SANDPAPER BEFORE GLUING.

DRILLING HOLES

Use the number-eleven X-ACTO blade or equivalent to drill holes where instructed. Place the tip at the point where you need a hole. Next twist the knife blade in ONE DIRECTION ONLY. This will result in a nicely rounded hole. Don't twist it back and forth. When the tip of the blade comes through the other side of the paper, stop. Turn the paper over and drill from the other side, using the same technique, until the hole is the desired size.

FORMING CYLINDERS

To allow paper to form a cylinder it is helpful to pre-bend it by drawing it across the edge of a counter or table top. Lay the piece of paper on a counter top near the edge. Next, place a book on top of it. Pull the paper across the edge of the counter and down at a 90-degree angle. Once you have pulled it all the way to the end, reverse the ends and repeat the procedure. You will find that the paper will now curl naturally.

TABS AND GLUING GUIDES

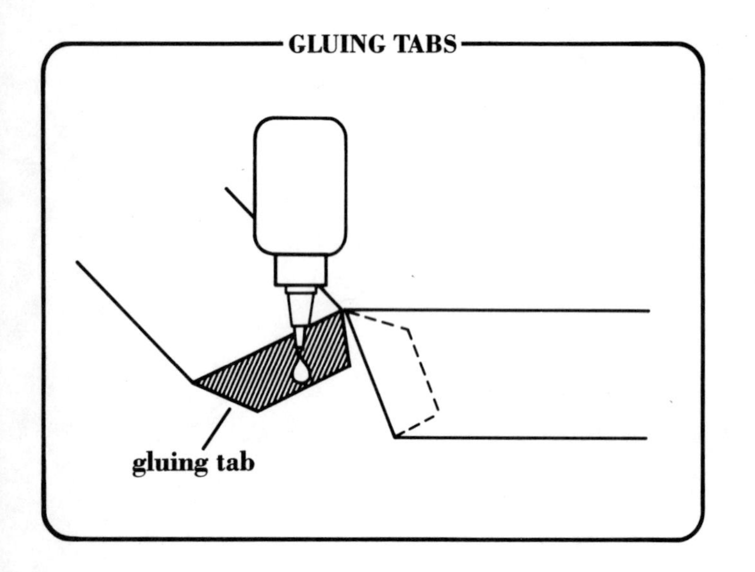

Tabs are bent and glued to another part to increase the strength of the model. They are shaded a dark color to identify them.

Gluing guides are areas marked with diagonal lines. They show you where another part will fit onto an area and indicate the approximate place where glue should be applied.

THE EXPLODED VIEW

An "exploded" view of the model is provided to guide you in construction.

EXPLODED VIEW

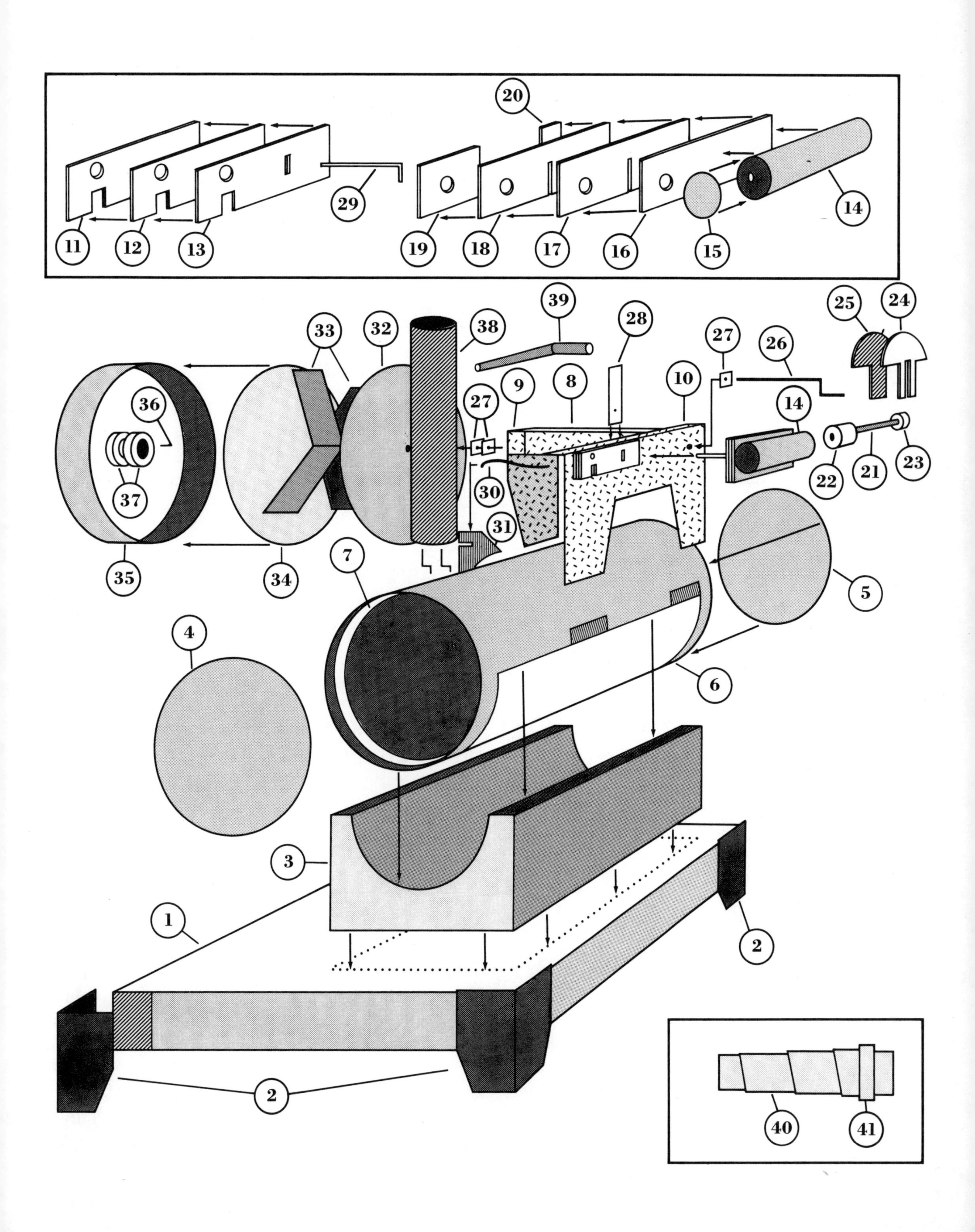

Study the exploded view closely before beginning work and refer to it often while building the model. It will let you see what each part is and will show you how the parts fit together. It is your most important aid for constructing the model.

BUILDING YOUR MODEL

BE SURE TO READ THE CONSTRUCTION TIPS AND STUDY THE EXPLODED VIEW OF THE MODEL BEFORE BEGINNING.

AS EACH STEP IS COMPLETED, CHECK THE BOX PROVIDED SO THAT YOU WILL BE BETTER ABLE TO KEEP TRACK OF YOUR PROGRESS.

AS YOU READ THROUGH THE INSTRUCTIONS, CONTINUE READING UNTIL YOU REACH A "STOP AND DO" SIGN. AT THAT POINT, STOP READING AND COMPLETE THE TASK JUST DESCRIBED.

STEP 1: Building the Engine Base

STEP 1.

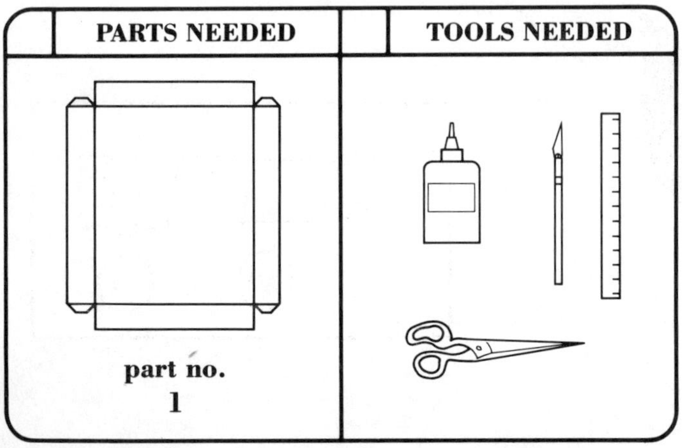

PARTS NEEDED	TOOLS NEEDED
part no. 1	

Part 1 will form the base for your model. Cut out part 1. Score and bend the sides *down* along the dotted lines. STOP AND DO.

Glue up part 1 (using white paper glue) by bending the tabs inward at the corners and applying glue only on the tabs, attaching them to the gluing guides. It will look like the lid of a shoe box when complete. STOP AND DO.

STEP 2: Attaching the Legs to the Base

The four parts labeled part 2 are the legs for the engine base. Cut out these four parts. Score and bend along the dotted lines. STOP AND DO.

Glue each of the base legs (part 2) to each corner of part 1. Make sure the narrow part of each leg extends beneath the base; the wide part aligns with top of base. Refer to the exploded view for placement of the parts. STOP AND DO.

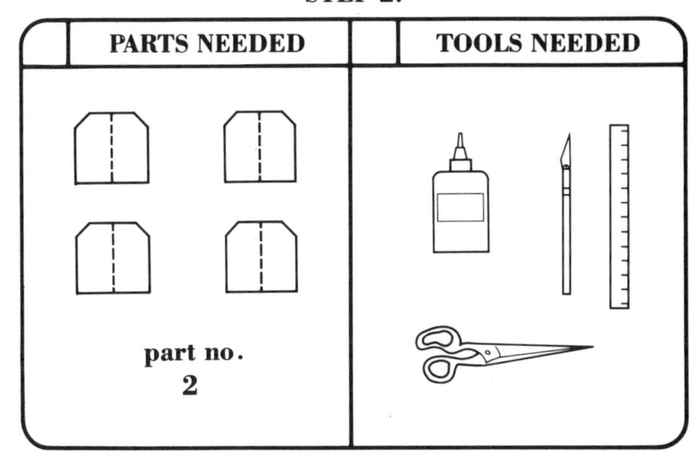

STEP 3: Building the Boiler Support

Cut out part 3, the boiler support. Score and bend along the dotted lines at the edges of the tabs and the edges of the white rectangle in the center. STOP AND DO.

Glue up part 3 so that the brick pattern appears on the outside. The four small tabs on the ends should be folded down and glued inside the engine support, underneath the ledge produced when the sides are folded. Remember to refer to the exploded view to see how part 3 goes together.

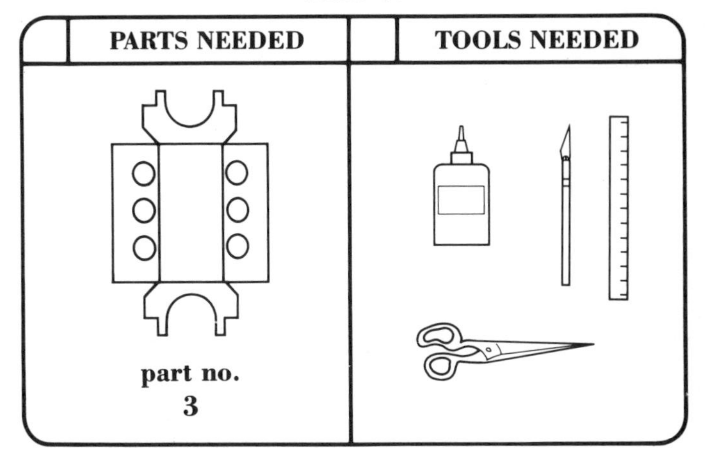

STEP 4: Gluing Boiler Support to Base

Glue part 3, the boiler support, onto part 1, the model base, where indicated. Notice that the end of the support that has the "fire door" goes on the opposite end to the smokestack location. STOP AND DO.

STEP 5: Building the Boiler

Cut out parts 4, 5, 6, and the two part 7s. STOP AND DO.

Use a needle to make a small hole at the places marked with "+" signs on part 6 and labeled A, B, C, and D. These holes will allow you to find these places on the back side of this part when you get to the next step. STOP AND DO.

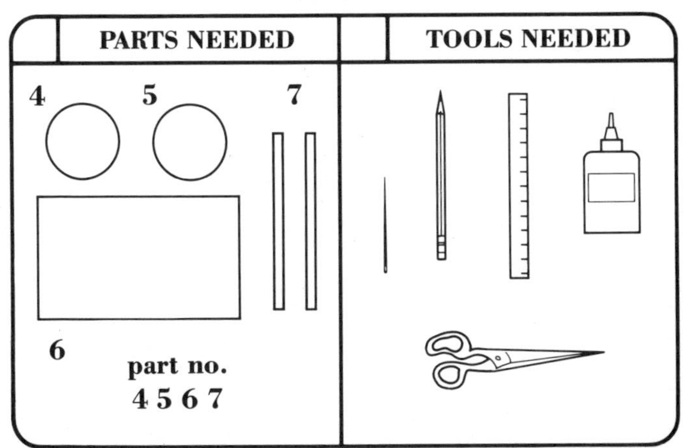

Turn part 6 over and use pencil and ruler to draw, on the back side, a line from A to B and a line from C to D. STOP AND DO.

The two part 7s are boiler end cap supports. They are not to be located at the edge of part 6. The two pencil lines you have drawn on the back of part 6 will show how far away from the edge of part 6 (back) you should glue the two part 7s. Glue the two part 7s in place, one at each of the pencil lines, using white glue. STOP AND DO.

Let the glue dry completely before proceeding.

Pull part 6 across the edge of a table to form a natural curl as explained in the construction tips on page 14. Pull vertically, from A to B, not from A to C. STOP AND DO.

Glue part 6 into a circle. Overlap the boiler only on the shaded glue area and glue EXACTLY. This overlap makes parts 4 and 5 fit perfectly. STOP AND DO.

When this glue is **completely dry,** you will find it easy to use your hands to smooth part 6 into a nice round shape. Work slowly and try to get any wrinkles smoothed out so that the boiler will have a nice appearance. STOP AND DO.

STEP 6: Gluing the Boiler Ends in Place

Put the first boiler end cap, part 4, into place but do not glue. Notice that it goes on the end of the boiler (part 6) that has the smokestack location marked. This stack location is the top of the boiler. Make sure that you install part 4 so that the picture is straight. STOP AND DO.

Put the other boiler end cap (part 5) into place on the other end of the boiler but do not glue. STOP AND DO.

With the boiler ends in place, run a bead of white glue around the outside edge of each piece to attach them permanently to the boiler. STOP AND DO.

Allow glue to dry completely before proceeding.

STEP 7: Installing the Boiler on the Boiler Support

Put the boiler you just built into place on the boiler support (part 3) but do not glue. Refer to the exploded view to make sure the smoke stack end of the boiler is in the right place (should be at opposite end from fire door). The markings on the boiler will help you get it lined up properly. STOP AND DO.

When the boiler is properly placed, apply white glue in six or eight spots where the boiler touches the support. STOP AND DO.

STEP 8: Building the Engine Support

Cut out, score and bend parts 8, 9, and 10. Cut out the two slots on part 10 which look like small white rectangles. Refer to the diagram on the right. STOP AND DO.

Glue together parts 8, 9, and 10 using the diagram below and the small arrows on parts 9 and 10 to get the parts lined up properly. Glue is added to end of part 8 and small area covered by lip on part 10. STOP AND DO.

This assembly will be called the "engine support." Allow glue to dry before proceeding.

STEP 8.

PARTS NEEDED	TOOLS NEEDED
8 9 10 part no. 8 9 10	

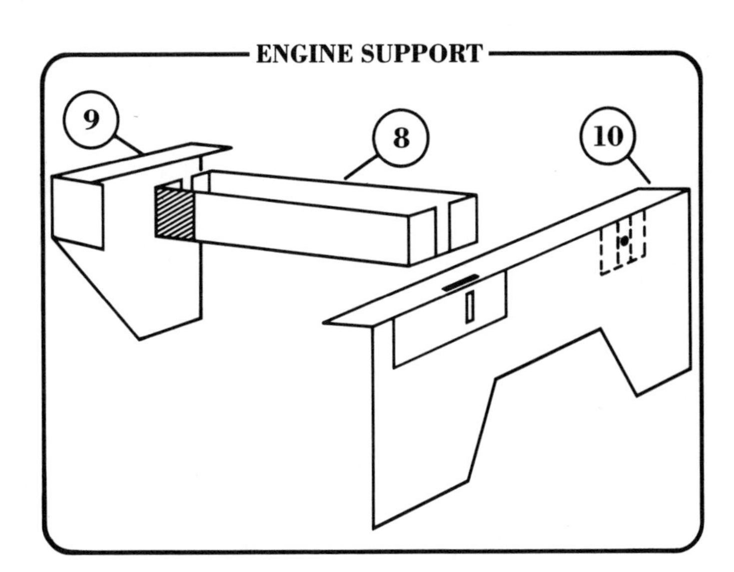

STEP 9: Installing the Engine Support

Refer to the exploded view and the diagonally shaded glue areas on the boiler (part 6) to glue the engine support in place on the boiler. It is important that you get it lined up properly. STOP AND DO.

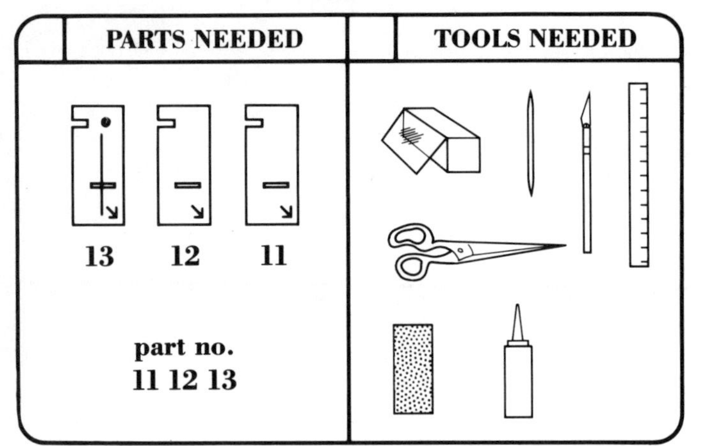

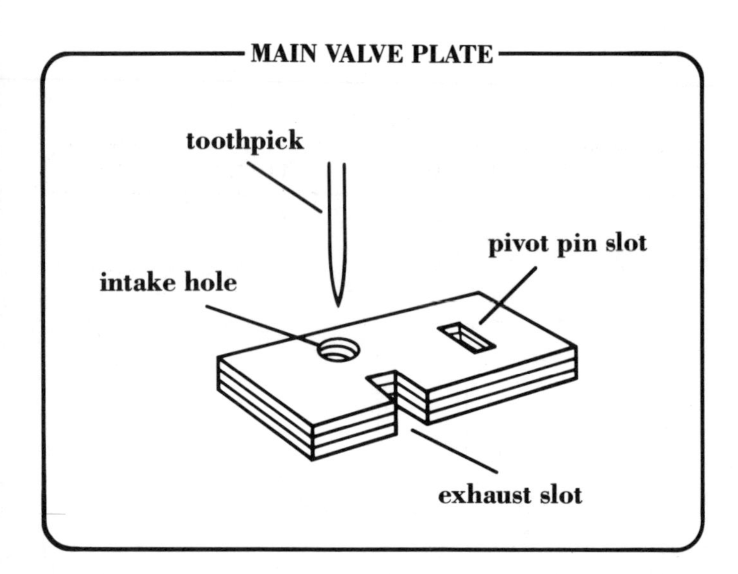

STEP 10: Building the Main Valve Plate

Parts 11, 12, and 13 will form the main valve plate. The valve plates are important parts of the engine. Instructions must be followed exactly to obtain best engine performance.

Be especially careful not to bend or otherwise deform these valve plates while working on them. **In this step you will be working with super glue. Be careful to keep the super glue off your fingers.**

Preparing the Parts

Cut out parts 11, 12, and 13. Use the X-ACTO knife to cut the pivot pin slot shown on the diagram on the left. STOP AND DO.

Place a sheet of waxed paper over your work surface. Stack parts 11, 12, and 13 together with part 13 on top (line facing up) and part 11 on bottom. When they are lined up exactly, apply a drop of super glue to the edges of the stack at each corner to hold them together while you allow the glue to set. STOP AND DO.

Gluing the Parts Together

Apply super glue carefully all around the edges of the assembly until the edges are wet. Place the assembly flat on the waxed-paper-covered work surface. Fold the waxed paper over the assembly to protect your fingers and press firmly to make sure the assembly stays flat while the super glue sets. STOP AND DO.

Remove the waxed paper from the top and apply super glue to the top surface of the assembly. Use another piece of waxed paper to protect your fingers and turn the assembly top down and rub on the waxed paper to spread the glue around. This is done to make sure the glue completely covers the surface and to help smooth the surface. Set the assembly aside until the glue has completely set. STOP AND DO.

When the glue is completely dry, place the valve plate flat on your work surface and use the X-ACTO knife to drill the intake hole. It is important that the intake hole is the right size. It should be just large enough to allow a round toothpick to pass through. STOP AND DO.

After drilling the intake hole, apply a small amount of super glue to the hole. This will stiffen the paper and allow you to shave away the ridge of paper formed around the hole by the drilling operation. Shave away the ridge when the glue has set. STOP AND DO.

Place a piece of sandpaper on a flat surface and place the valve plate assembly flat on the piece of sandpaper. Sand lightly to remove any rough spots. Turn the assembly over and sand the other side. **Be careful not to bend the valve plate or round off the edges while sanding.** STOP AND DO.

STEP 11: Installing the Main Valve Plate

Drilling the Intake Hole in Part 10

The main valve plate just completed will be glued onto part 10. Its location is shown by the diagonally shaded glue area on part 10. Refer to the diagram on the right to see how to locate it. It is important that it is glued onto part 10 correctly. Do not glue yet.

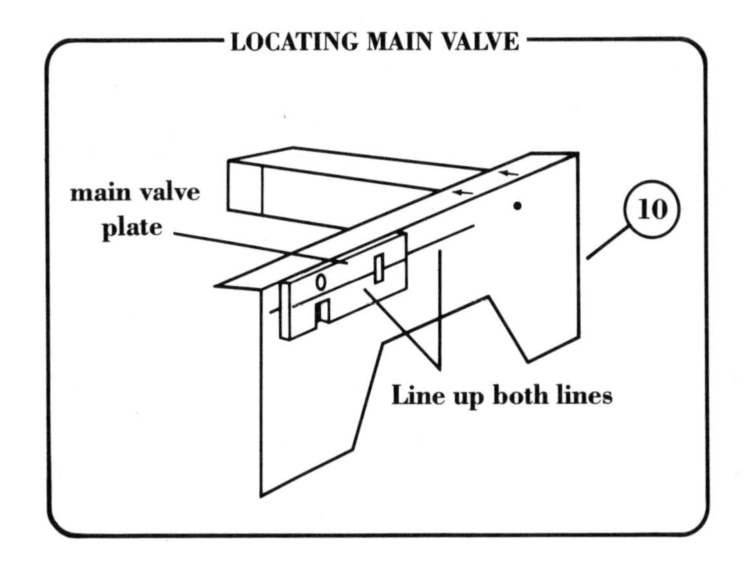

Notice that the slot you cut in part 10 should line up with the slot you cut in the main valve plate. Notice also that the black line on the main valve plate should line up with the black line on part 10.

Before gluing the main valve plate into place you must mark and drill the intake hole in part 10. Hold the main valve plate in place and push a needle through the intake hole in the valve plate and through part 10 to mark the location to drill the intake hole in part 10. STOP AND DO.

Drill the intake hole in part 10 large enough to allow a round toothpick to pass through it. STOP AND DO.

Shave away any ridge around the hole made by the drilling operation so that the surface is left flat. STOP AND DO.

Gluing the Main Valve Plate onto Part 10

Use white glue to glue the main valve plate onto part 10. Make sure that it is lined up correctly. STOP AND DO.

Check to see that the intake hole has not been stopped up by any extra glue. If necessary, use the hobby knife as a drill to clean out the intake hole. Be careful not to damage the smooth surface of the main valve plate. STOP AND DO.

STEP 12: Building the Engine Cylinder

STEP 12.

PARTS NEEDED	TOOLS NEEDED
15 14 part no. 14 15	

Preparing the Parts

Cut out parts 14 and 15. STOP AND DO.

These parts will form the engine cylinder. Notice that one end of part 14 has a shaded glue area. Place part 14 face up on waxed paper.

Apply several drops of super glue to the back side of this area, fold the waxed paper over the part and rub so that the super glue is spread evenly and completely wets this area. STOP AND DO.

When the super glue has set, sand both sides of this area lightly to leave a smooth surface. STOP AND DO.

Forming the Engine Cylinder

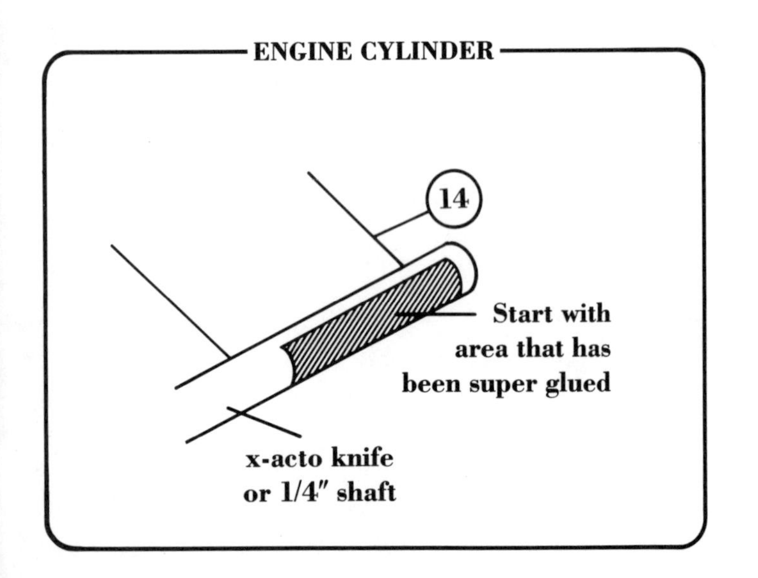

First, pull part 14 across the edge of a table lengthwise several times to give it a natural curl. STOP AND DO.

Wrap part 14 around the handle of your hobby knife (or a one-quarter-inch shaft) to form the cylinder. Begin with the glued end of part 14 and wrap toward the dotted end. Keep the wraps tight and even. When the wraps are complete, use white glue on the end of the last wrap to hold it in place. Refer to the diagram on the left. STOP AND DO.

When this glue is dry, carefully slide the cylinder until it is half way off the end of the knife handle. Now apply a few drops of super glue to the outside of the cylinder and use a small piece of waxed paper to spread the glue all around the outside of the cylinder to wet the entire surface. *Be extremely careful not to allow the super glue to come into contact with the knife handle. Otherwise you will be unable to remove the cylinder without distorting its shape*. STOP AND DO.

When the glue is completely set, carefully remove the cylinder from the knife handle. STOP AND DO.

Glue the cylinder end cap, part 15, onto one end of the cylinder using white glue. STOP AND DO.

When the glue is dry, blow gently into the open end to check for air leaks. If a leak is found, plug with white glue or apply baking soda to the area, dust lightly with a Q-tip, then apply super glue.

Apply a small amount of super glue around the edge of the open end of the cylinder to stiffen it. This will also form a small ridge just inside the cylinder opening. Use the knife blade to very gently scrape away this ridge once the glue has set. STOP AND DO.

Drilling the Intake Hole in Cylinder

Handle the cylinder carefully so as not to deform it when working on it. Refer to the diagram on page 22 to drill the intake hole at the proper point on the cylinder. The hole should be just large enough to allow a round toothpick to pass through it. STOP AND DO.

STEP 13: Building the Cylinder Valve Plate

The cylinder valve plate is made in much the same way as the main valve plate was made in step 10. Refer to step 10 to refresh your memory. STOP AND DO.

Cut out parts 16, 17, 18, 19, and 20. Cut out the slot on part 17 and on part 18 but do not drill the intake hole in any of these parts at this time. Refer to the diagram on the next page. STOP AND DO.

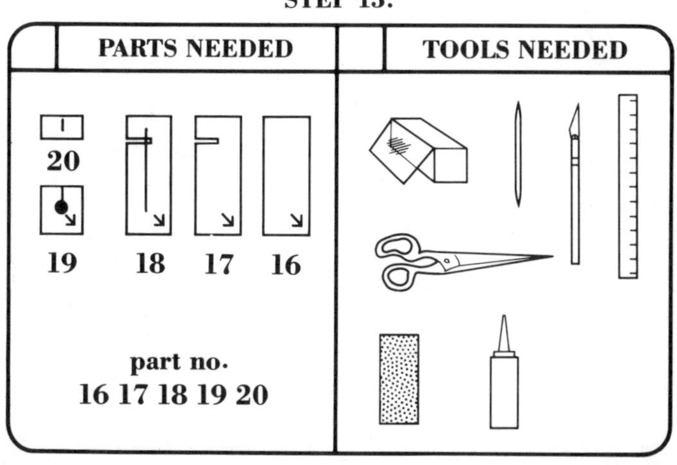

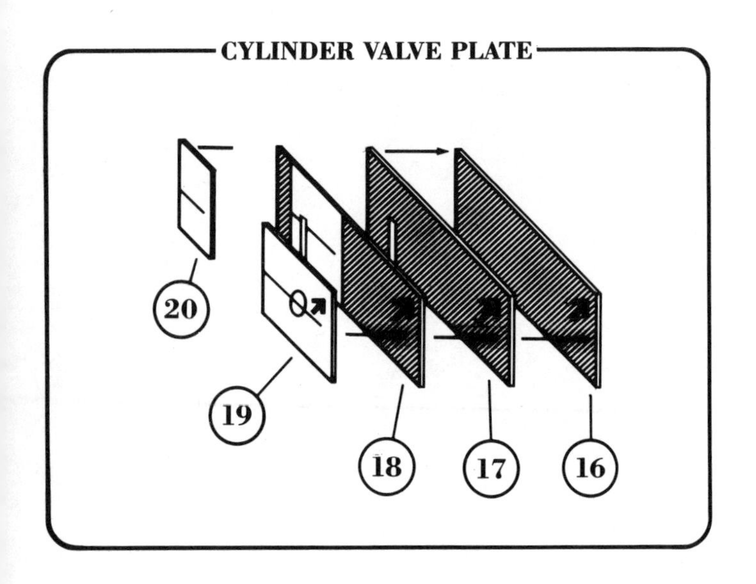

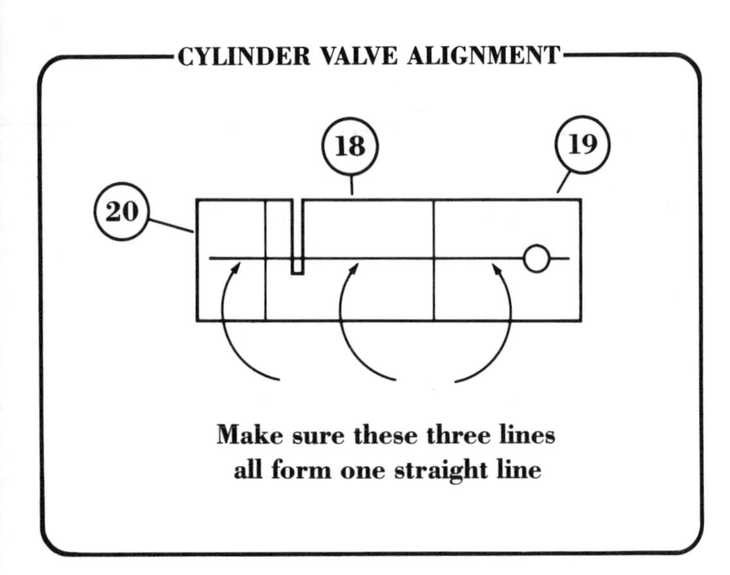

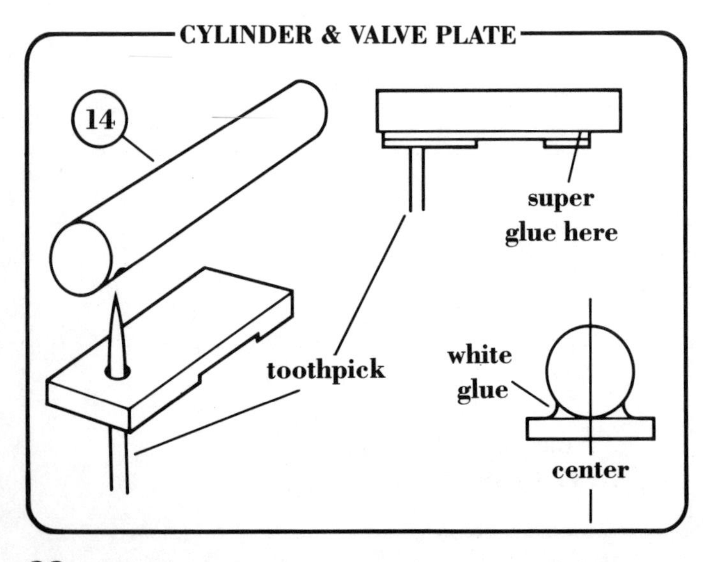

Stack parts 16, 17, and 18 together with part 18 on top. Line them up carefully and glue them together as in step 10 (apply a drop of super glue to the edge at the four corners. When this glue has set, place the assembly flat on a piece of waxed paper and apply super glue all around the edges. Fold the waxed paper over the part to protect your fingers and press down to keep the assembly flat while the glue sets). STOP AND DO.

Refer to the diagram on the upper left and glue parts 19 and 20 in place using **white** glue. The correct placement of parts 19 and 20 on part 18 is important. The markings on parts 18, 19, and 20 will help you line up the parts correctly. Study the diagrams carefully. STOP AND DO.

When parts 19 and 20 are in place and the glue has completely set, apply several drops of super glue to their front surfaces, turn them face down on waxed paper, and rub to spread the glue around to leave a smooth surface. STOP AND DO.

When the glue has completely set, put the assembly face down on a piece of fine sandpaper and sand lightly to get a smooth surface. STOP AND DO.

Next drill the intake hole shown on part 19 using the same technique used on the main valve plate (see page 19). Drill the hole large enough to pass a round toothpick through it. STOP AND DO.

Put a drop of super glue in the hole but make sure that excess glue does not block the hole. Shave away the ridge left by the drilling operation, then sand lightly by placing the part face down on a piece of fine sandpaper laid flat on a table. STOP AND DO.

Finally, use the knife blade to clean out the hole to toothpick size. STOP AND DO.

STEP 14: Attaching the Cylinder Valve Plate to the Cylinder

Refer to the drawing on the left for placement of the cylinder valve plate on the cylinder. Use a toothpick pushed through the intake hole in the cylinder valve plate and then into the intake hole in the cylinder to line them up. The bottom (part 16) should face the cylinder. To glue the valve plate onto the cylinder, first apply two drops of super glue to the cylinder where the parts will touch and away from the toothpick. Hold the parts together until the glue sets while keeping them lined up as in the drawing on the right. STOP AND DO.

When the glue has set, gently remove the toothpick. STOP AND DO.

Check the parts to see if they are lined up properly. If they are, use the end of a toothpick to apply white glue all around the area where the cylinder and the valve plate touch. *Let this glue dry completely before handling the cylinder assembly again*. STOP AND DO.

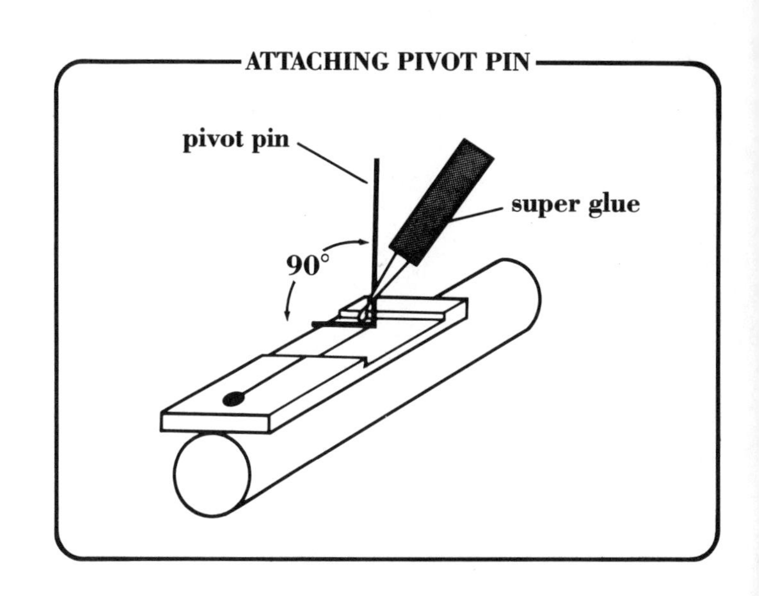

Attaching the Cylinder Pivot Pin

Cut and bend a paper clip to form part 29, the cylinder pivot pin. Use the bending guide provided. STOP AND DO.

Glue the pivot pin onto the cylinder valve plate using super glue. The short end of the pin fits into the slot in the cylinder valve plate. Dusting with baking soda helps in filling around the pin. Super glue should be reapplied after doing this. Be careful not to get glue on the flat surface of the valve plate. Refer to the diagram below. STOP AND DO.

STEP 15: Building the Piston and Piston Rod

Preparing the Parts

Cut out parts 22 and part 23. Notice that there are two parts labeled part 22. STOP AND DO.

Make part 21 from a round toothpick using the cutting guide provided. STOP AND DO.

Pull the two pieces of part 22 across the edge of a table to give them a natural curl. STOP AND DO.

STEP 15.

PARTS NEEDED

22 23 21

part no.
21 22 23

TOOLS NEEDED

Building the Piston

Wrap one of the part 22s around one end of the toothpick to begin forming the piston. Keep the wraps as tight and as even as possible. Use white glue to hold the last wrap in place. STOP AND DO.

Continue wrapping the second piece of part 22 right on top of the first piece where it stopped but with no overlap. Check the size of the piston as you wrap this piece, stopping the wrap when a slightly loose fit inside the cylinder (piece 14) has been attained. Cut off the unused part of piece 22 and apply a very small amount of white glue to temporarily hold it in place. STOP AND DO.

Check the fit of the piston in the cylinder. It should be a loose fit so that the piston will drop **freely** to the bottom of the cylinder. If necessary, add or remove **one wrap** at a time until a good fit is achieved. STOP AND DO.

Wrap part 23 around the opposite end of the toothpick to form what will look like a small piston. Glue the final wrap with white glue. STOP AND DO.

Apply super glue to each end of the piston. The super glue should be applied at all edges of the paper and around the outside surfaces so that all paper parts are wet. Use a scrap of waxed paper to wipe excess glue and leave a smooth surface. STOP AND DO.

When the super glue has completely set, hold the piston assembly at the middle, wrap a small piece of fine sandpaper around the piston (part 23) and rotate the piston to smooth and polish it. Check the fit of the piston in the cylinder again and continue to polish with sandpaper if necessary until the piston moves freely in the cylinder. STOP AND DO.

Use the hobby knife to drill a hole in the small end (part 23) of the piston rod. Drill first one side and then the other. Make the hole large enough for the crankshaft end (this is paper-clip width; crankshaft will be built in step 16) to pass freely through it. The hole should go right through the paper and the wood. Refer to the diagram on the right. STOP AND DO.

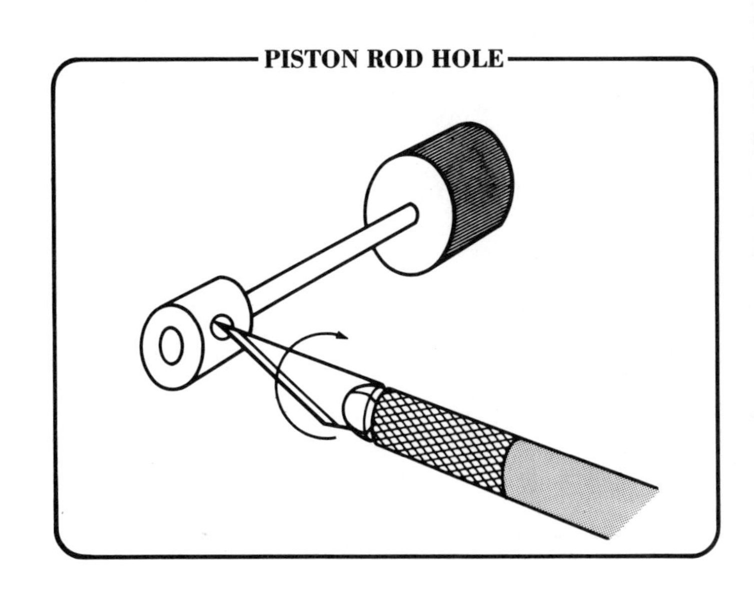

STEP 16: Building the Counterweight and Crankshaft

Making the Counterweight

Parts 24 and 25 will form the counterweight for the engine crankshaft.

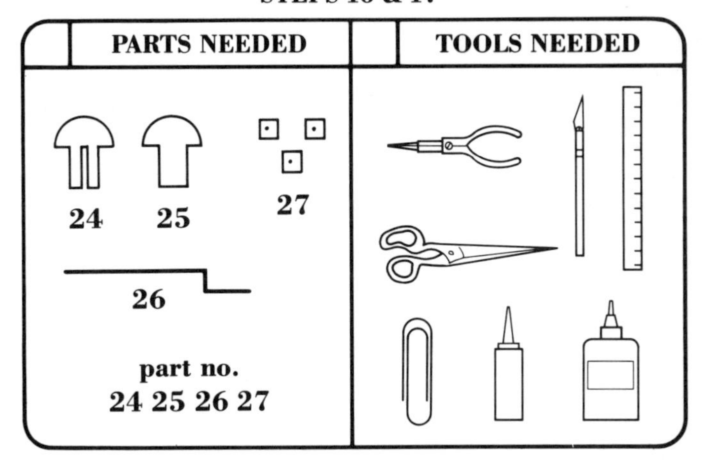

Cut out parts 24 and 25. STOP AND DO.

Drill a hole at the dot on part 25. Make it just large enough to let a small paper-clip wire pass through it. STOP AND DO.

Use white glue to glue parts 24 and 25 together back to back. STOP AND DO.

Making the Crankshaft

The crankshaft (part 26) is made from a paper clip. First select a paper clip (a small one if you have more than one size) and straighten it out. It needs to be as smooth and straight as you can get it. Use your needle-nose pliers if desired, and keep working on it until it is nice and straight. (You can check it for straightness by rolling it on a flat surface.) STOP AND DO.

When you have it straightened to your satisfaction, use the bending guide provided to bend it into the shape of the crankshaft. Use the needle-nose pliers to make nice sharp bends. Double check to make sure it has the right shape and, if necessary, cut it to the proper length. STOP AND DO.

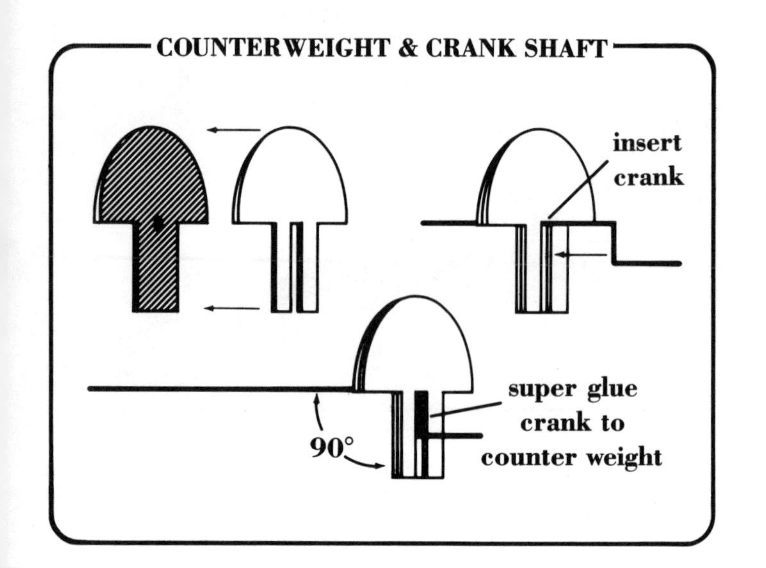

Assembling the Counterweight and Crankshaft

Refer to the diagram on the left to see how the crankshaft fits into the counterweight. Make a trial fit and when you are satisfied, use one drop of super glue to secure the crankshaft into place on the counterweight. STOP AND DO.

When that glue has set, double check to see that the crankshaft is lined up as the diagram shows. Then add more super glue to make the joint between the crankshaft and the counterweight strong. STOP AND DO.

STEP 17: Installing the Crankshaft Assembly

Notice that there are three parts labeled part 27. Cut out these three parts and drill a hole in each one at the indicator dot. Make the hole just large enough to pass a small paper-clip wire through it. STOP AND DO.

These parts will serve as spacers to make the crankshaft run smoothly. Install the crankshaft assembly into the engine support (at the hole in part 10), placing the spacers (parts 27) as shown in the exploded view. STOP AND DO.

STEP 18: Installing Parts 28, 30, 31, and the Cylinder Assembly

Part 31 provides a place to attach one end of part 30 which is made from a rubber band. The rubber band acts as a valve spring to hold the cylinder valve plate against the main valve plate. Part 28 is provided to make sure that proper valve alignment is obtained; do not glue part 28 at this time.

STEP 18.

PARTS NEEDED	TOOLS NEEDED
28 30 31 part no. 28 30 31	

Preparing the Parts

Cut out part 31. STOP AND DO.

Cut out part 28 and drill a hole large enough to fit a small paper-clip wire at the place indicated by a dot. STOP AND DO.

Make part 30 by cutting out a two-inch-long piece of a very thin and weak rubber band. STOP AND DO.

Installing the Parts

Glue part 31 onto the side of the boiler (part 6) using white glue. There is a stripe on the boiler to help you put it in the right place. Look at the diagram on the right and at the exploded view to see how it fits onto the boiler. STOP AND DO.

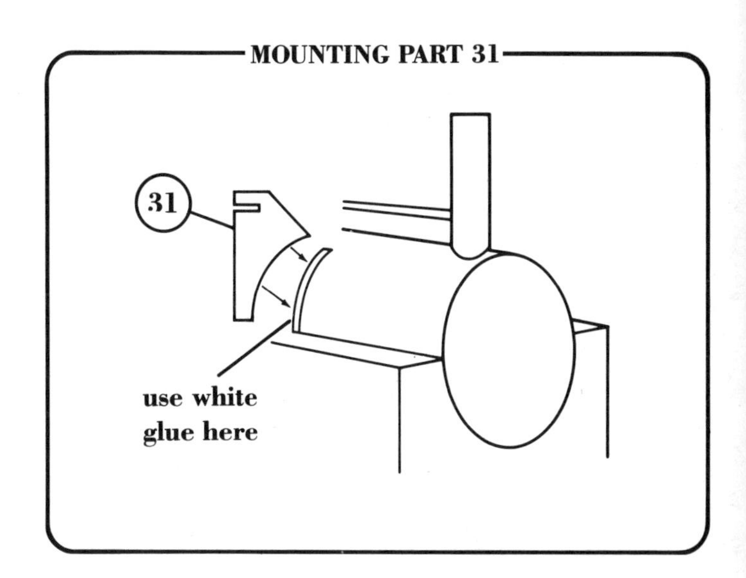

Slide part 28 into the slot in the engine support which is part 10. Refer to the diagram below. STOP AND DO.

Install the cylinder assembly. The pivot pin (part 29) which was previously attached to the cylinder assembly goes into the slot on the main valve plate (parts 11, 12, and 13) and then through the hole that you drilled in part 28. Look at the drawing on the right to see how these parts fit together. STOP AND DO.

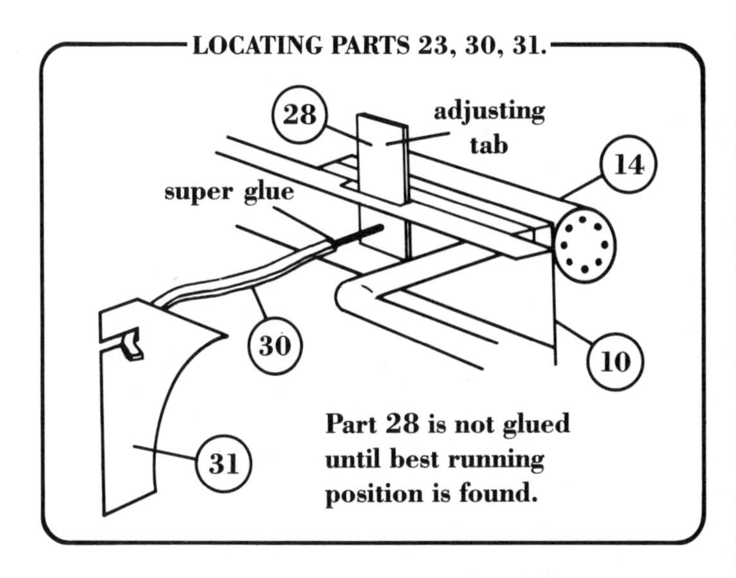

With the cylinder assembly in place, put the smallest possible drop of super glue on one end of the rubber band (part 30) and attach it to the end of the pivot pin (part 29). Look at the drawing below. STOP AND DO.

Attach the other end of the rubber band by pulling it through the slot in part 31. THE RUBBER BAND SHOULD BE VERY LOOSE IN ORDER TO ALLOW THE ENGINE TO RUN PROPERLY. Work carefully to get it just tight enough to keep the cylinder valve plate against the main valve plate. DO NOT INSTALL THE PISTON AT THIS TIME.

STEP 19: Building the Flywheel

Preparing the Pieces for Assembly

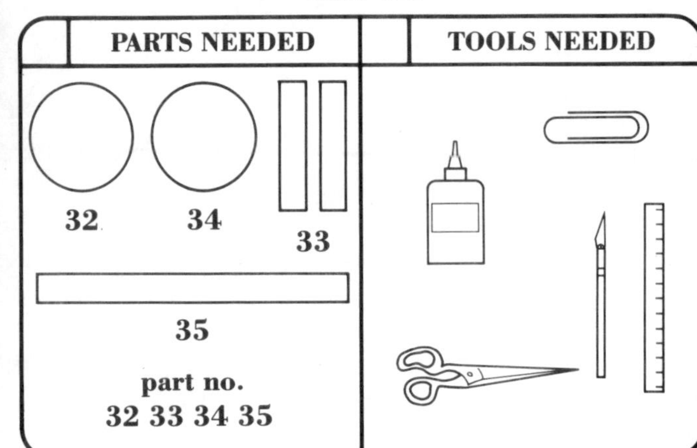

Cut out parts 32, 33, 34, and 35. STOP AND DO.

First make the outer rim of the flywheel from part 35. Pull part 35 across the edge of a table to form a natural curl. STOP AND DO.

Make part 35 into a circle. The ends must overlap just enough to cover the shaded glue area on one end of the part. Use white glue only on the shaded glue area. STOP AND DO.

There are two parts labeled part 33. Score these on the dotted line and bend to a 90-degree angle. STOP AND DO.

Drill a hole in the center of part 32 and in the center of part 34. Make these holes just large enough to let a small paper-clip wire pass through them. STOP AND DO.

Place part 32 face up on your work surface. Glue first one part 33 in place and then glue the other part 33 in place using white glue. The lines on part 32 will show you where to glue these parts. Notice that these lines do not touch each other in the center of part 32 and neither should the two part 33s. This will leave room for the crankshaft to pass through the flywheel. STOP AND DO.

Assembling the Pieces of the Flywheel

Refer to the exploded view to see how the flywheel fits together.

Lay the flywheel rim (part 35) on the work surface and fit the assembly made of parts 32 and 33 inside with part 32 on the bottom. It should be a tight fit and you must work carefully to push it down into the rim so that the back side is flush with the edge of the rim. If it slips out of the rim, start over. STOP AND DO.

When you are satisfied with the fit, glue these parts together by turning the assembly face down and applying a small bead of white glue around the edge of part 32 where it touches the rim. STOP AND DO.

Next place the flywheel on the work surface, face up, and fit part 34 into place on top. STOP AND DO.

When you are satisfied with the fit, glue part 34 by applying a thin bead of glue around its edge where it touches the rim of the flywheel. STOP AND DO.

STEP 20: Building the Drive Pulley

Parts 36 and 37 will be used to make a small pulley which will fit onto the crankshaft next to the flywheel.

STEPS 20 AND 21.

PARTS NEEDED	TOOLS NEEDED
36 37 part no. 36 37	

Preparing the Parts

Cut out parts 36 and 37. Notice that part 37 is two pieces. STOP AND DO.

Pull the three pieces you just cut out across the edge of a table to form a natural curl. STOP AND DO.

Putting the Pieces Together

Study the diagram on the right to see how the drive pulley is made.

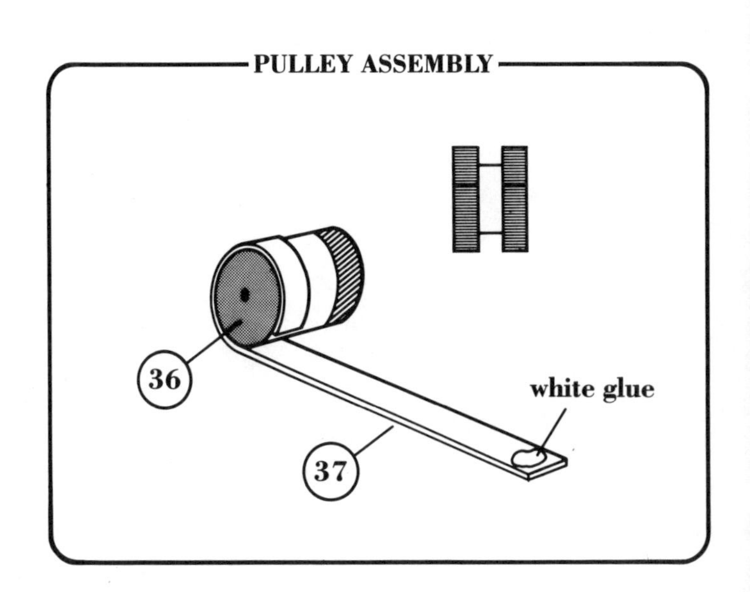

Roll part 36 into a tight roll to form a small, solid cylinder (leaving a hole about the size of a small paper-clip wire) and glue with white glue. STOP AND DO.

Each of the part 37s will be rolled around one end of part 36 so as to leave a space between them. This will form a groove in the finished drive pulley. The width of this groove is indicated by the white strip on part 36. Refer to the diagram above and roll and glue onto part 36 (with white glue) each of the part 37s. STOP AND DO.

STEP 21: Installing the Flywheel and Drive Pulley

Make sure the spacers you previously installed on the crankshaft are still in place. Slide the flywheel onto the crankshaft as shown in the exploded view. STOP AND DO.

Place a drop of super glue on the crankshaft where it sticks out of the flywheel. This will hold the flywheel in place on the crankshaft temporarily. STOP AND DO.

Place several drops of super glue into the center of the circle of the drive pulley (parts 36 and 37) and slide it onto the crankshaft so that it is firmly against the flywheel. The super glue will hold the drive pulley in place on the flywheel and will also hold the flywheel in place on the crankshaft. STOP AND DO.

STEP 22.

PARTS NEEDED | TOOLS NEEDED

38 41

part no.
38 41

STEP 22: Building the Smokestack

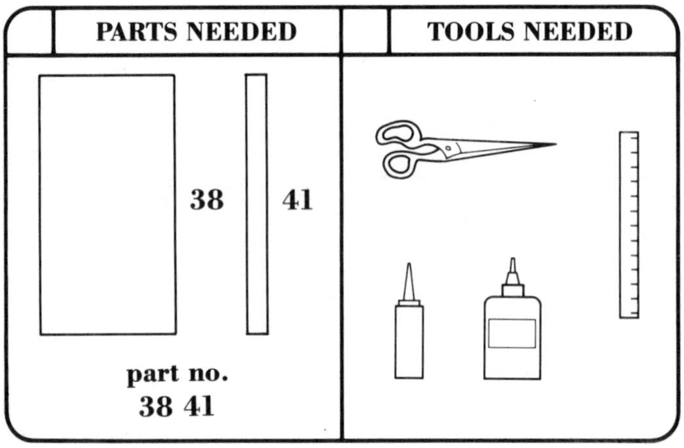

The smokestack is made from part 38.

Preparing the Parts

Cut out parts 38 and one of the part 41s. STOP AND DO.

Pull parts 38 and the one part 41 across the edge of a table lengthwise, one at a time, to give it a natural curl. STOP AND DO.

Putting the Parts Together

One end of part 38 has a shaded area which will show you how much overlap you need when you roll it into a cylinder shape to form the smokestack. Start with the shaded end of part 38 and carefully roll it into a cylinder shape. Use white glue at the very end of the final wrap to hold it in place. STOP AND DO.

Put super glue around the top end of the smokestack. (The top end of the smokestack is the end with double black lines.) You should apply enough super glue to get the paper wet (both inside and outside) down to the double black lines. This will make the top of the smokestack both strong and waterproof. Roll the one part 41 around the stack, along the double black lines. This will form a reinforcing band. STOP AND DO.

STEP 23: Building the Air Tube

Preparing the Part

Cut out part 39 and pull it across the edge of a table to give it a natural curl. STOP AND DO.

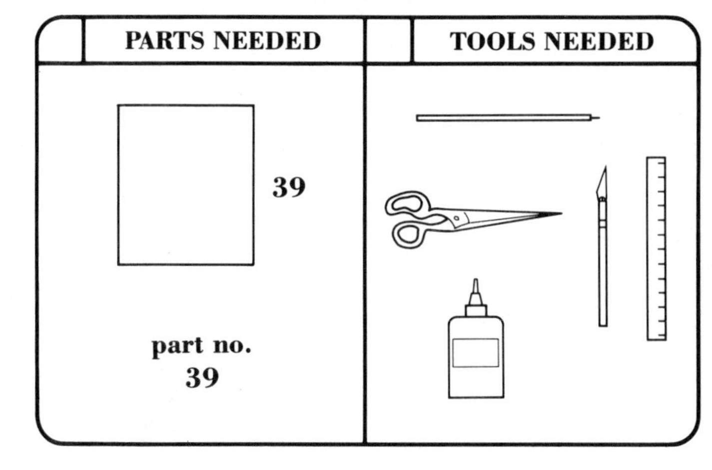

You will use a ballpoint-pen refill as a form for making the air tube. Roll part 39 tightly around the tube of the pen refill. Use white glue on the edge of the last wrap to hold it in place. STOP AND DO.

When the glue is dry, slide the air tube off the refill tube and place the newly formed air tube on the cutting guide and cut carefully as shown. STOP AND DO.

Glue the two pieces of the air tube together at a 90 degree angle (like the corner of a picture frame). Make sure that the glue doesn't block the air tube. STOP AND DO.

Installing the Smokestack and the Air Tube

Drill a hole in one side of the smokestack right at the single black stripe. Make the hole big enough to put the air tube into it. STOP AND DO.

Use scissors to trim the bottom of the smokestack to fit the boiler. You should trim only a very small amount of the stack away. **Be sure to trim the stack so that the hole you drilled for the air tube faces the opposite end of the boiler when the stack is in place.** STOP AND DO.

Glue (with white glue) the smokestack into place on the boiler. Refer to the exploded view and the markings on the boiler to see where it goes. STOP AND DO.

When the glue is completely dry on the smokestack, glue the air tube into place at both ends. Refer to the exploded view. Notice that the long end of the air tube goes into the hole you drilled in the smokestack and the short end goes in line with the intake hole on the main valve plate. STOP AND DO.

When the glue has completely dried on the air tube, check the intake hole on the main valve plate to make sure it is not blocked by excess glue. Also check for air leaks at the joints of the air tube. STOP AND DO.

STEP 24: Building the Balloon Holder

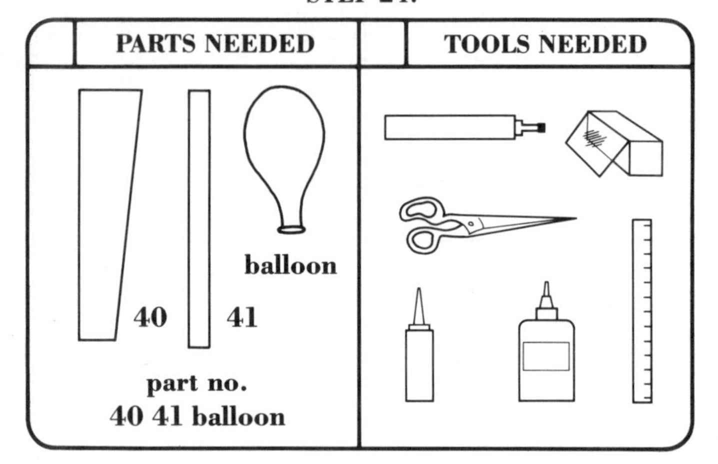

Use parts 40 and the second part 41 to make the balloon holder. It will serve as a nozzle which will fit into the open end of the smokestack so that the balloon will provide the air pressure to make your "steamless steam engine" run.

Cut out part 40 and pull it across the edge of a table to give it a natural curl. STOP AND DO.

Roll part 40 into a tube. It should form a tapered tube that will fit snugly part way into the open end of the smokestack (tapered end first). Glue the last wrap with white glue. STOP AND DO.

Cut out the remaining part 41. STOP AND DO.

Roll part 41 around part 40 to form a reinforcing band at the black stripe on part 40. Glue the last wrap with white glue. STOP AND DO.

Check the fit of the balloon holder you just made. It should fit snugly into the smokestack. STOP AND DO.

Use a piece of waxed paper wrapped loosely around the balloon holder to hold it while you apply super glue. Work carefully to make sure the super glue does not come into contact with your hands. Apply enough super glue to wet all parts of the balloon holder both inside and out and including the reinforcing band. STOP AND DO.

TESTING YOUR STEAMLESS STEAMER

Install the large piston (piece 22) in the cylinder and slide the crankshaft through the hole in the small end of the piston rod. STOP AND DO.

Check the exploded view and the check boxes by each step in the instructions to make sure all parts are assembled correctly.

When you are satisfied, it is time for a test run.

First apply a small amount of graphite powder into the open end of the engine cylinder and between the valve plates. This will lubricate the engine for smoother running.

Install a balloon on the balloon holder. Pull the open end down over the reinforcing band so that it will stay on. Blow up the balloon and use the first two fingers (not the thumb) to pinch the neck of the balloon while you insert the balloon holder into the smokestack.

Release the balloon and turn the flywheel very gently to start the engine running. It should run for 30 seconds or more with a good balloon.

Do not be disappointed if the engine does not run on the first attempt. There are several things to check and several adjustments you can make to get your engine running or to improve the way it runs. Read *Trouble-shooting and Tuning Your Engine* to determine what adjustments to make.

If you want to give your steam engine the true test, you can build a table saw that can be run on the power from your engine.

STEP 25: Construction of Table Saw

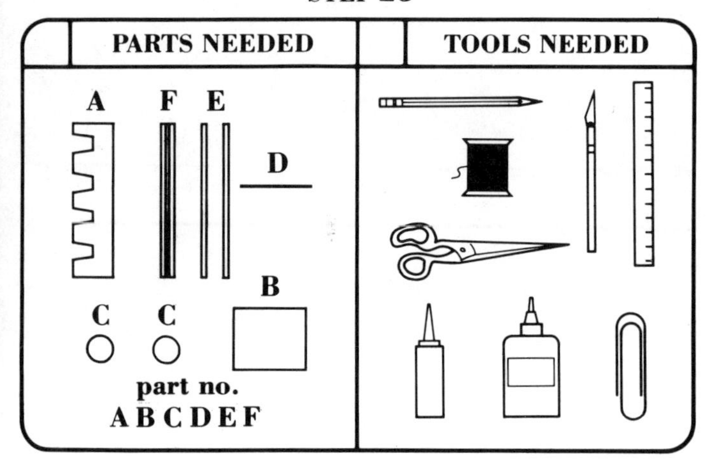

Cut out part A. Score on the dotted lines. Form into a square stand and glue tab inside. Refer to the exploded view for shape. STOP AND DO.

Cut out part B. Cut and remove the slot in the very center of this part. STOP AND DO.

Cut out the two parts labeled part C. Glue them back to back, using white glue. STOP AND DO.

With an X-ACTO knife, drill the two holes in part A where indicated. Use a sharp pencil and twist it in the holes to make smooth, round holes that will accommodate a paper clip. The lead from the pencil will leave graphite in the hole for lubrication. STOP AND DO.

With an X-ACTO knife, drill the hole in the center of part C, drilling wide enough to accommodate a paper clip *snugly*. STOP AND DO.

Straighten a paper clip and cut it to length using guide D. STOP AND DO.

Cut out the two parts labeled E and part F. Construct a pulley as you did in step 20 by first pulling parts E and part F lengthwise across the edge of a table to form a curl. Roll part F tightly to form a small, solid cylinder, and glue with white glue. STOP AND DO.

Wrap each of the part Es around each end of part F, leaving a space in between them (see page 31). This will form a groove in the pulley. STOP AND DO.

Now glue each of the part Es onto part F, using white glue. STOP AND DO.

Pass the axle (the paper clip) through the hole in part A, from the outside. Place part C on the axle, inside the stand that is part A, and push the axle through the other hole in part A. Position part C in the center of part A. Make sure enough of the axle sticks out of part A— $\frac{1}{4}$ inch on one side and $\frac{5}{8}$ inch on the other side. STOP AND DO.

Test-fit part B on top of part A, making sure part C, the blade, is centered in the slot on part B. Remove part B and glue part C to the axle with super glue. Rotate the blade and adjust until there is no wobble. STOP AND DO.

Place white glue on the top lip of part A and place part B on top of part A, making sure part C comes through the slot on part B. STOP AND DO.

Take the assembled drive pulley (parts E and F) and place on the $\frac{5}{8}$-inch end of the axle. Push the axle into the center of the pulley and glue with super glue. STOP AND DO.

Cut about 14 inches of sewing thread and tie the ends together in a square knot. Put a small amount of white glue on the knot and roll it between your thumb and index finger. This makes the drive belt. STOP AND DO.

Put the drive belt around the steam engine pulley and the table saw pulley. Set them far enough apart to draw the thread tight. STOP AND DO.

Now blow up your balloon and watch your engine make your table saw run!

Tip: If your saw moves too close to the steam engine while running, add weight to the saw (tape a couple of pennies inside the base).

TROUBLESHOOTING AND TUNING YOUR ENGINE

If your engine does not run on the first attempt, the following suggestions may solve your problem.

1. Some balloons are unusually weak. If this is your problem, you can find out by simply blowing directly into the smokestack. If the engine runs after turning the flywheel, then you have been using a weak balloon. If this is the case, one solution is to use two balloons by putting one balloon inside another. Remember that it is usually necessary to give the flywheel a gentle spin to start the engine.
2. Check the tension of the valve spring (rubber band). It should be just tight enough to keep the cylinder valve plate in light contact with the main valve plate. Try reducing the tension. You will probably think it is too loose when it is correctly adjusted.
3. Check the surfaces of the main valve plate and the cylinder valve plate to see if they are smooth. A raised area around the inlet hole caused by the drilling operation or a drop of glue spilled on these surfaces can prevent the engine from running well. If they are not smooth, the best way to correct the problem is as follows.

   With the cylinder still in place, slip a piece of fine sandpaper between the two valve plates. Work the sandpaper back and forth while holding the two valve plates lightly together. Reverse the sandpaper and repeat the procedure.

   Check the surfaces again and if they are smooth, blow away the dust that remains and apply more graphite powder.
4. Check the air tube for air leaks. Plug leaks with white glue. Check the air tube, the inlet hole in the main valve plate, and the inlet hole in the cylinder valve plate to make sure they are not blocked.

5. Check the fit of the piston in the cylinder. It should drop freely to the bottom of the cylinder when released. Also check to see that the cylinder has not been deformed or otherwise damaged. You might like to try inserting the handle of the hobby knife into the cylinder to make sure it is still round.
6. Check the flywheel and the crankshaft for freedom of movement. Make sure they are not rubbing against another part of the engine. The flywheel should turn freely and it should coast several turns when given a very gentle spin by hand. Remember that too much tension on the rubber band or rough and uneven valve plates will also keep the flywheel from spinning freely.
7. Check the alignment of the inlet hole in the main valve plate with the inlet hole in the cylinder valve plate according to the diagram in the instructions. Adjust part 28 (the pivot pin adjusting plate) as necessary to get proper alignment and glue it in place with white glue. Part 28 is a timing device; moving it very slowly up and down will compensate for any minor misalignment. This must be performed while engine is running.
8. Check the end of the crankshaft that passes through the small end of the piston. Make sure that the end of the crankshaft is smooth and that the bend in the crankshaft is properly made.
9. It is possible that after running your engine numerous times, the moisture from your breath will begin to accumulate in the engine. This can cause the engine to run poorly. If this happens, simply set the engine aside. It will run well again when it has had a short time to dry out.

It is suggested that the same balloon not be used day after day. This suggestion is made for health considerations and because after numerous inflations, a balloon will tend to become weaker.

CARE OF YOUR MODEL

Your steamless steam engine should last almost indefinitely and provide many hours of entertainment. It needs only minimal care. Add graphite powder occasionally to keep it well lubricated. Handle it gently and keep it in a safe place.

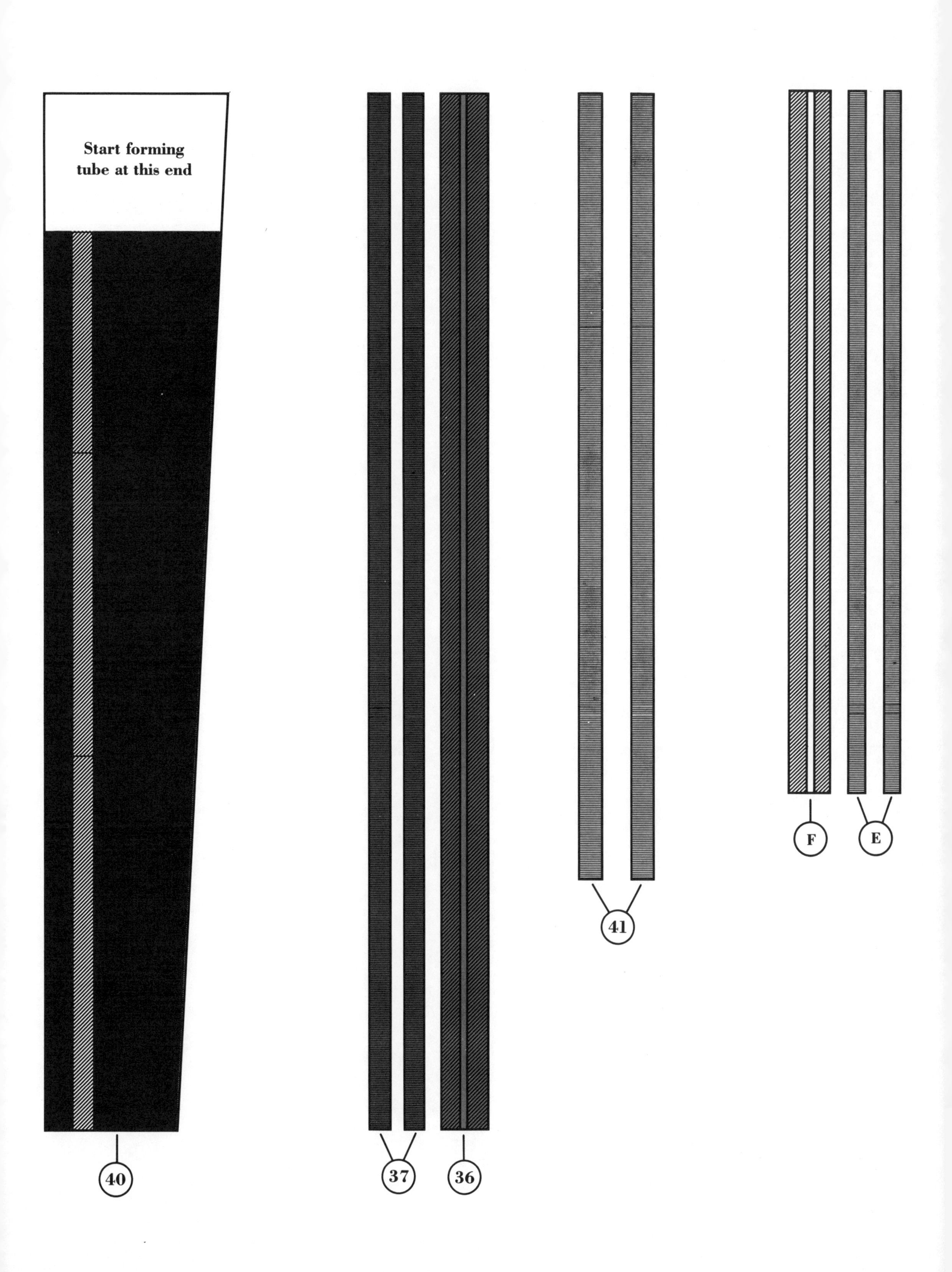
Start forming
tube at this end
40
37
36
41
F
E

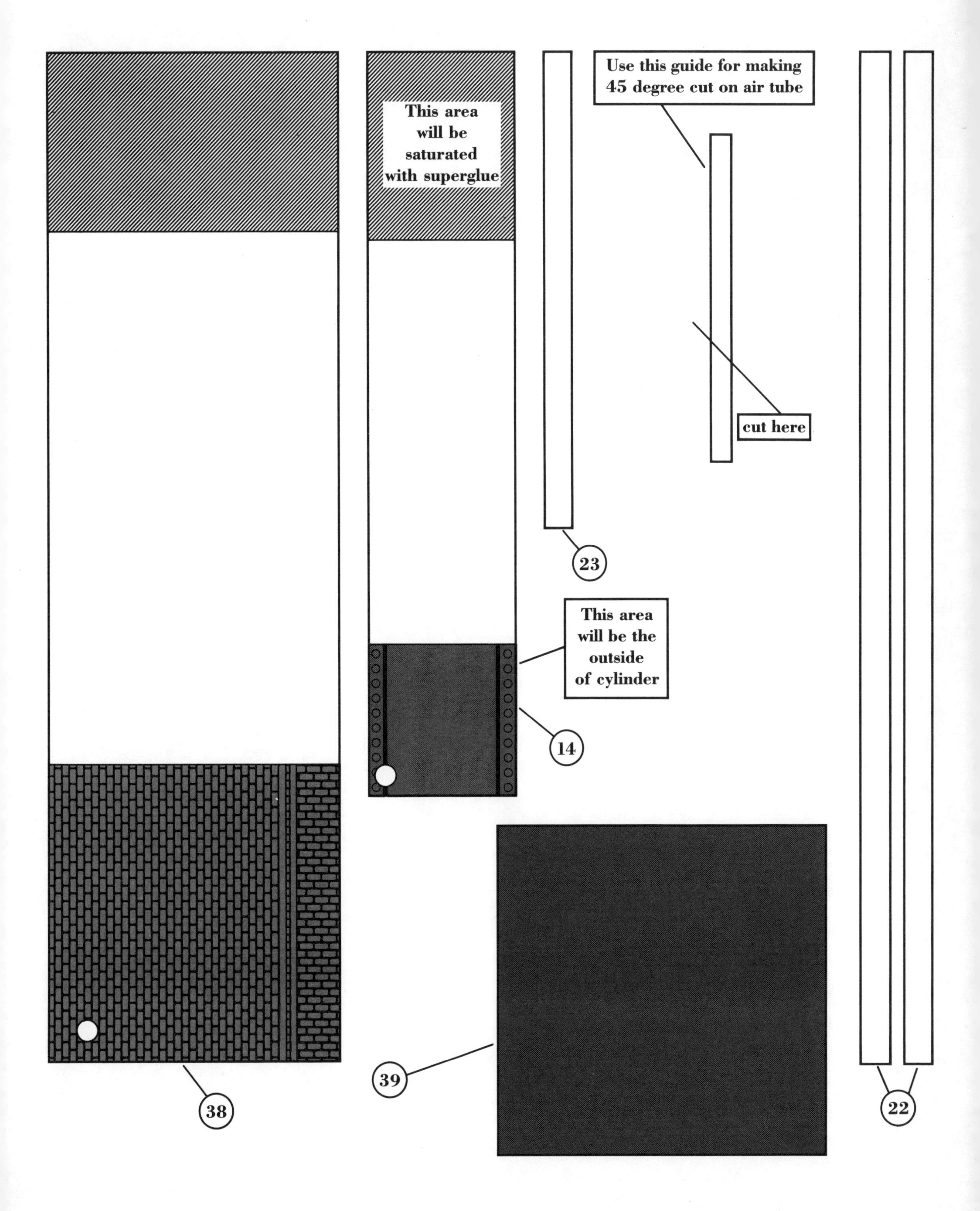
This area
will be
saturated
with superglue
Use this guide for making
45 degree cut on air tube
cut here
23
This area
will be the
outside
of cylinder
14
38
39
22

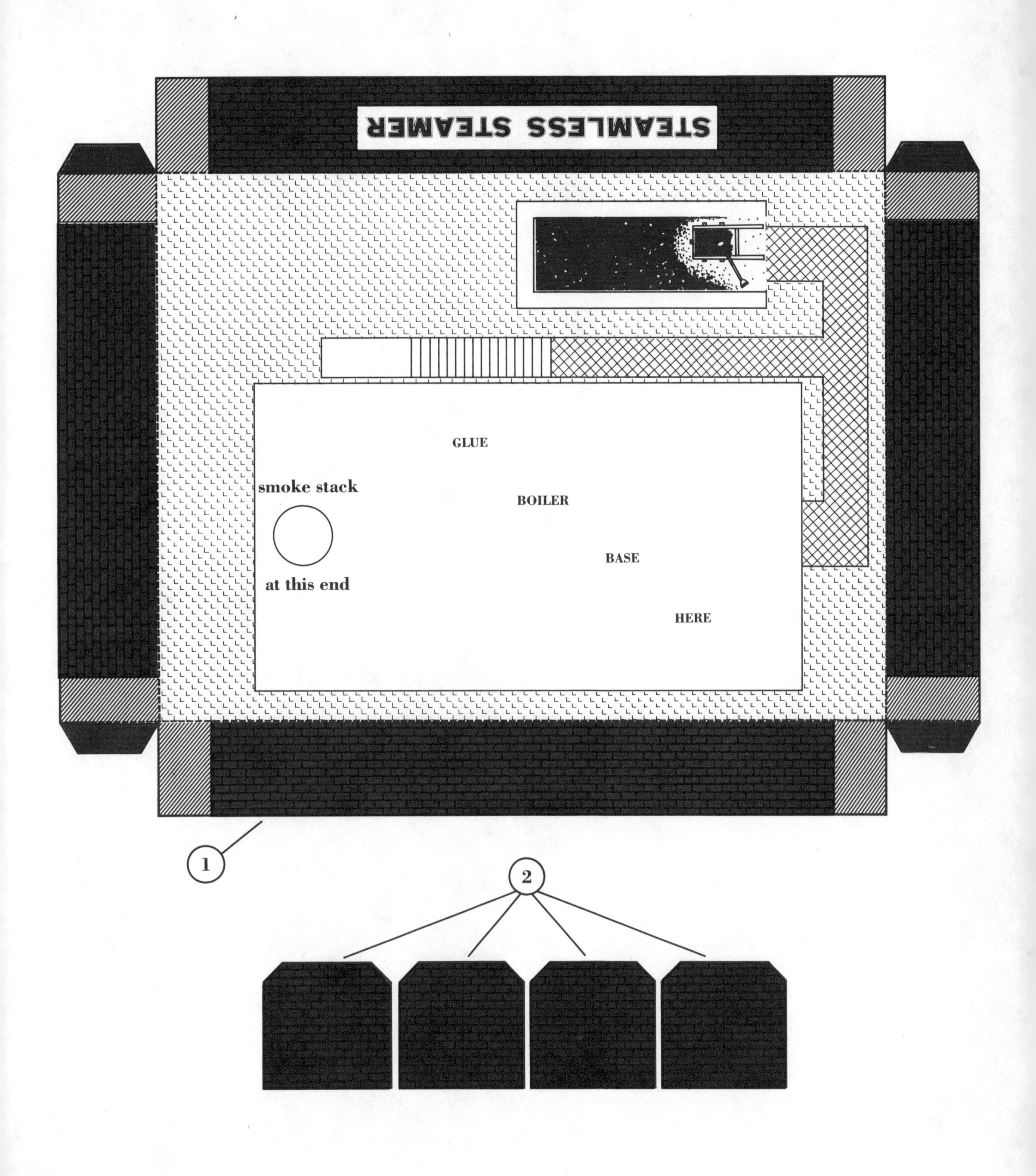
STEAMLESS STEAMER
GLUE
BOILER
BASE
HERE
smoke stack
at this end
1
2

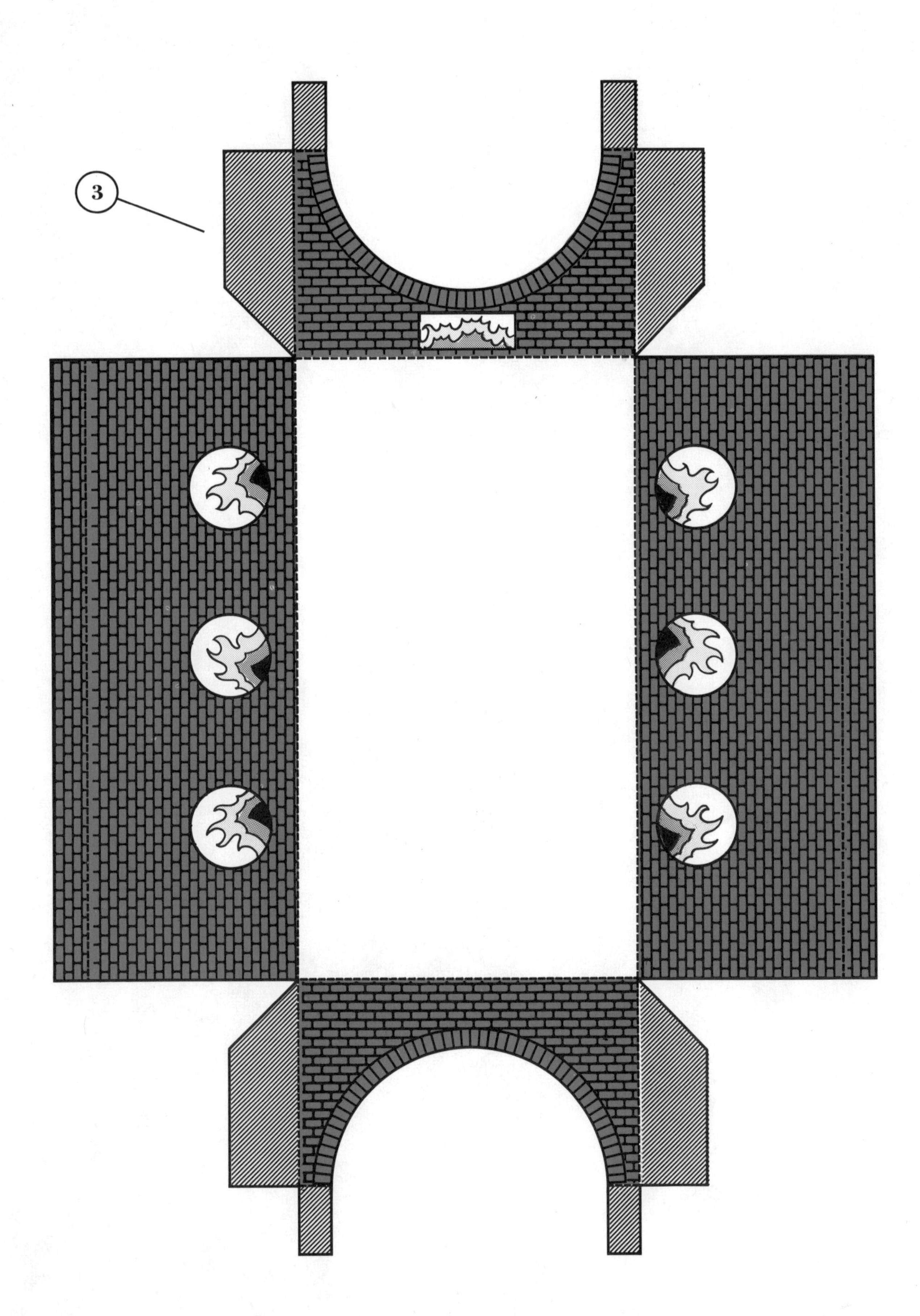
3

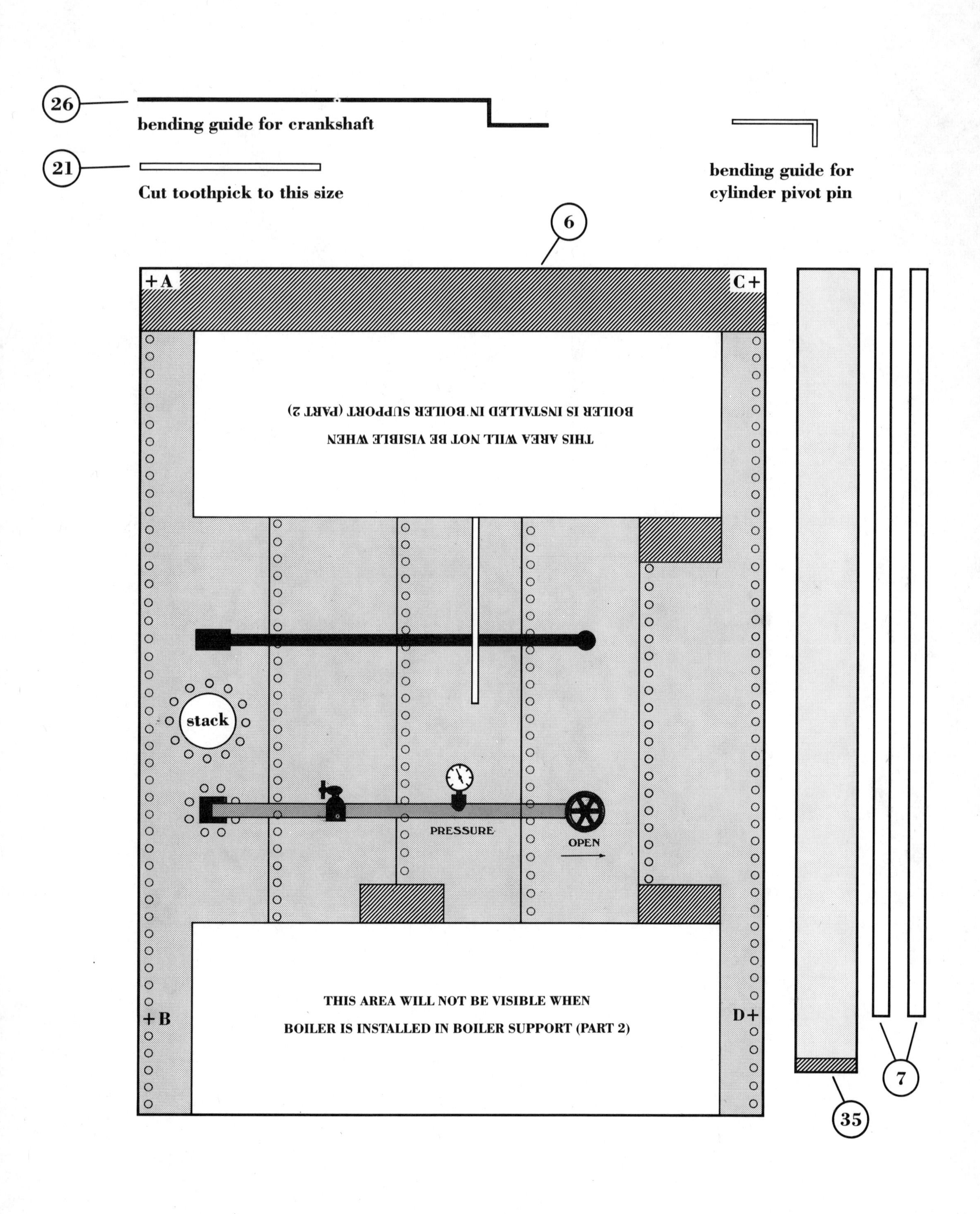
26
bending guide for crankshaft
21
Cut toothpick to this size
bending guide for
cylinder pivot pin
6
+A
C+
THIS AREA WILL NOT BE VISIBLE WHEN
BOILER IS INSTALLED IN BOILER SUPPORT (PART 2)
stack
PRESSURE
OPEN
THIS AREA WILL NOT BE VISIBLE WHEN
BOILER IS INSTALLED IN BOILER SUPPORT (PART 2)
+B
D+
35
7

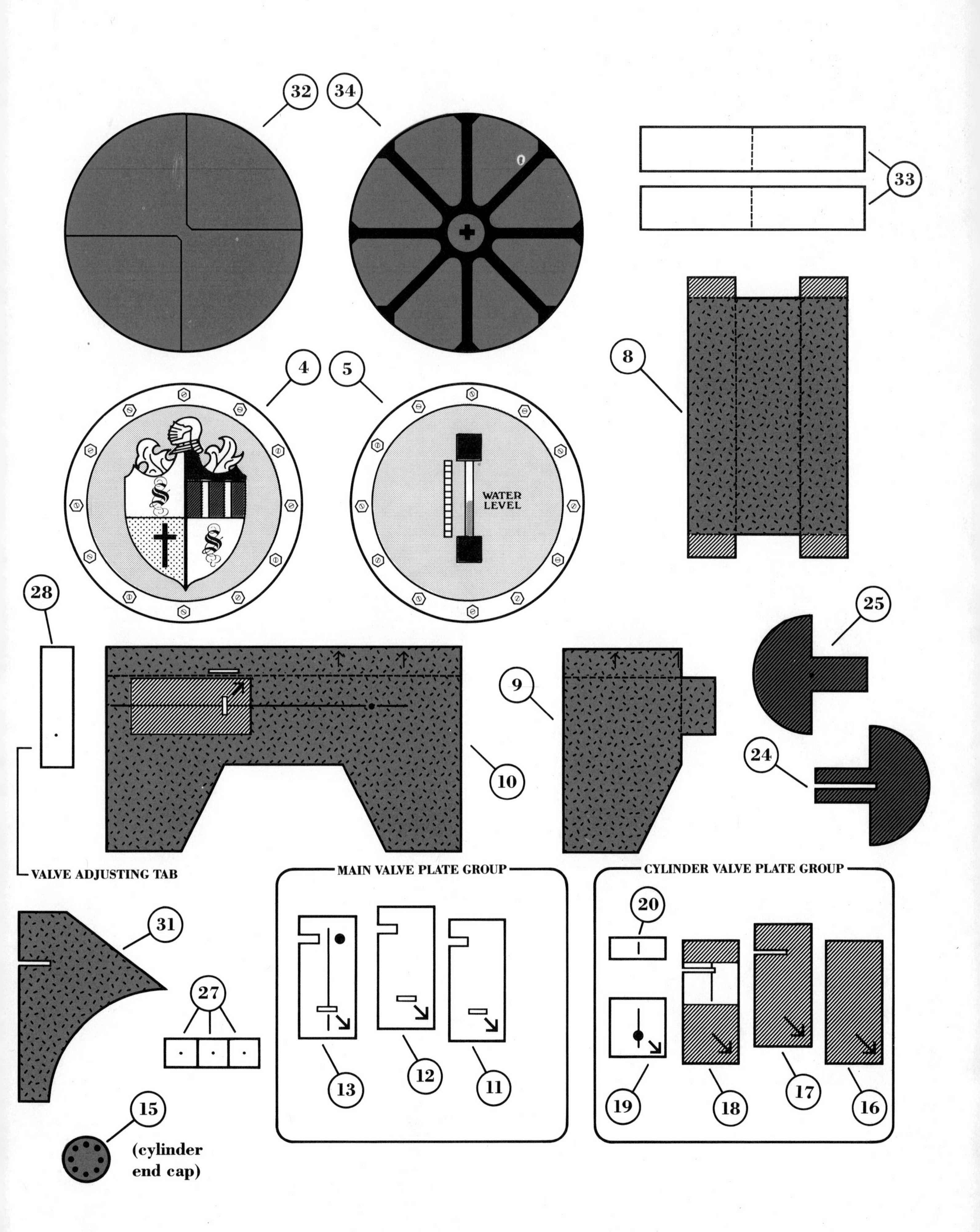
32
34
33
8
4
5
WATER LEVEL
28
25
9
10
24
VALVE ADJUSTING TAB
MAIN VALVE PLATE GROUP
CYLINDER VALVE PLATE GROUP
20
31
27
13
12
11
19
18
17
16
15
(cylinder end cap)

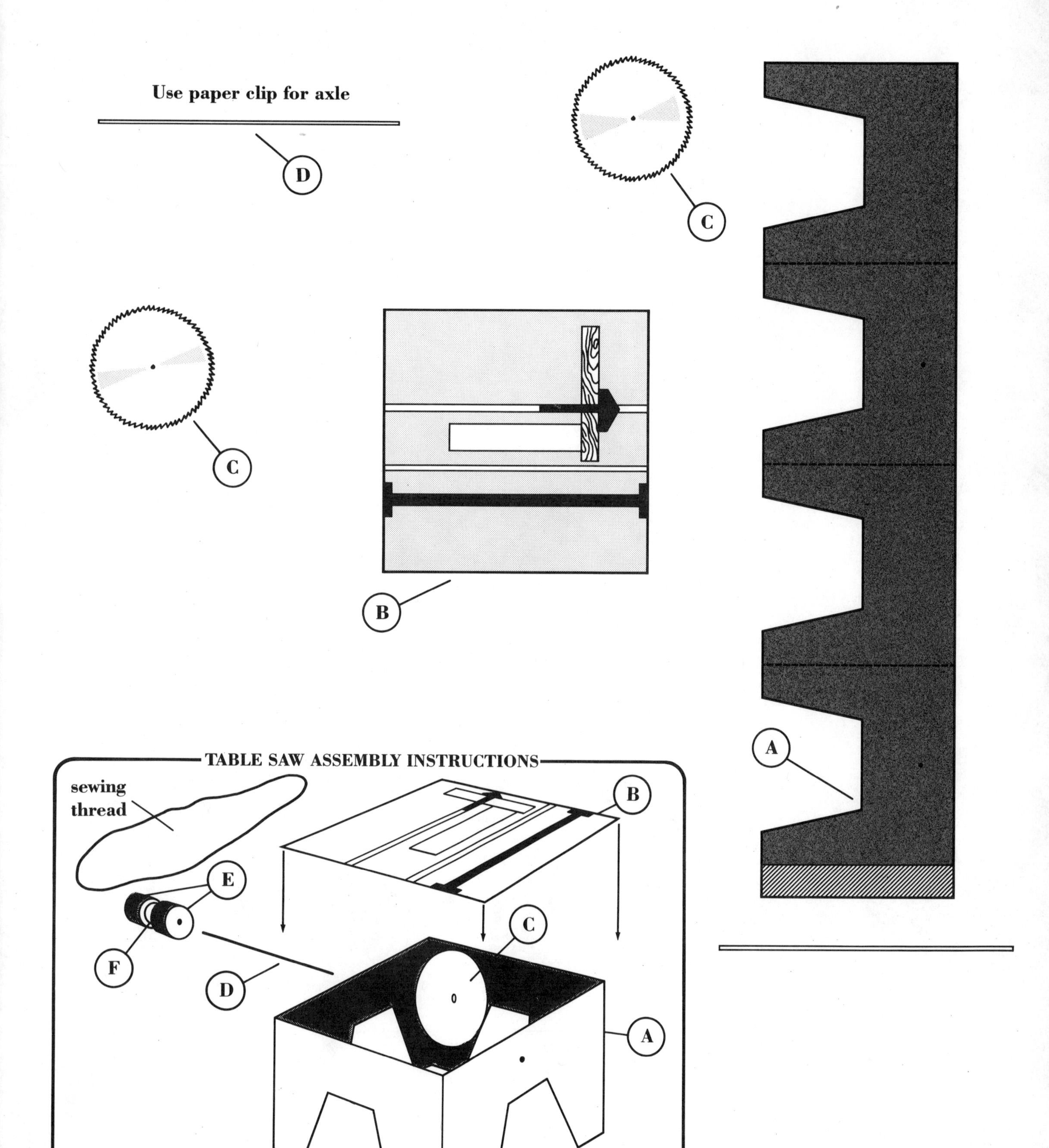
Use paper clip for axle
D
C
C
B
A
TABLE SAW ASSEMBLY INSTRUCTIONS
sewing thread
B
E
F
C
D
A